A Shift in Leadership

(Formerly titled *Leadershift: Transitioning from the Pastoral to the Apostolic)*

John Eckhardt

Foreword by: Bishop Nicholas Duncan-Williams

A SHIFT IN LEADERSHIP

John Eckhardt

CRUSADERS MINISTRIES
Oak Park/Chicago, Illinois
U.S.A.

Unless otherwise indicated, Scriptural quotations are from the **KING JAMES VERSION** of the Bible.

Indicated Scriptural quotations and translations in addition to those from the **KING JAMES VERSION** of the Bible are from:
THE WORD: The Bible from 26 Translations

A SHIFT IN LEADERSHIP
Published and Produced by:
Crusaders Ministries
P.O. Box 0469
Oak Park, IL 60303
ADBA: Crusaders Ministries
Crusaders Church (of Chicago)
Chicago, IL

A SHIFT IN LEADERSHIP - Formerly titled *Leadershift: Transitioning from the Pastoral to the Apostolic;*
ISBN 1-883927-14-5.

ISBN 1-883927-24-2

Printed in the United States of America (U.S.A.)

CMC-C/FBAO
08/2005

Contents

Foreword

There is a shifting in the spirit, and the body of Christ is in a time of crucial transition. If the potential leaders in the body of Christ today are going to make the impact expected of them by God, we must become prophetically compliant to what God is saying in the now. My dear friend, Apostle John Eckhardt has received a strong prophetic word from God for the present leadership in the Church, worldwide. Friend, I believe that the cloud has shifted, and there will come sudden changes in leadership within the body of Christ, worldwide. This is why this publication by Apostle Eckhardt is so strategic and crucial.

We must realize that change is of the essence. In Genesis, God clearly told Abraham to *sacrifice Isaac,* yet later told him *not to touch the lad.* Did God change His mind? No. God spoke a word to Abraham for a specific time and purpose, and He spoke another timely word to Abraham for another purpose. God didn't want Isaac; He wanted Abraham's heart. He is the same God that told David to ambush the Philistines in one instance and later instructed David not to go after them, but rather to change the strategy.

God in one instance told the prophet Elijah to *go to the brook and drink and be fed by ravens.* In another instance, He told him to *go to the widow of*

Zarephath and there you will be sustained. What am I saying?

I am saying that we must be a people who learn to hear what God is saying in this hour. If we act on yesterday's word alone, we might miss God. If we are willing to give God our Isaac, He is more than willing to give us Jesus. He wants to give us more of the presence of Jesus in the Church, but it will not come without the inclining of our ears to hear *what thus saith the Lord.*

The future of the Church hangs in the balance of whether the present leadership will sacrifice its notions of keeping potential apostles in the pastoral office, glued to the pulpits that make them secure. There are thousands of pastors who are not responding to the apostolic call for fear of what their congregations, or even worse, what other pastors will think. They believe that if they are absent from the pulpit for any length of time, the people will leave the church.

Jesus clearly states that He would build His church and that the strategies of hell would not stand against it. So, why don't we obey God and let Him build His church through us, whether your congregation is 50 or 50,000? It has been said that change is the proof of trust. If we truly trust the Lord to build His church, we would change our ways of thinking.

What I am stating here is not some esoteric, theological notion that looks good on paper. I am talking about actually changing your geographical location to affect cities and nations throughout the world through good, old-fashioned obedience to Christ. I am talking about leaving the realms of comfort in order to see the Scriptures come to life in your churches and ministries. I am talking about living lives of sacrifice and embracing the apostolic office to the point of shattering the religious mind-sets which literally kill men and women of God through the overbearing demands of the sheep in the fold.

Friend, realize that God is a *progressive* God. Whatever the shift of God's emphasis might be, we must not be fearful of the unknown or the unfamiliar. For some, it could be the moving to another geographical location, but for others it might be a change of emphasis. *The moving from one mantle to the next is where the conflict lies and where many find the greatest challenge in making the transition.* This could be one of the causes of strife in church leadership, financial lack, and even marital struggles. This was the case of Lot. The Lord was bringing Lot out of Sodom, and his wife wasn't willing to make the change. Many leaders will have to employ the grace of God to bring their spouses to the place of understanding the transition.

It is better to obey God and finish your course, like the Apostle Paul did, with controversy, than to live without controversy, having the acceptance of men, and not finish your course. The problem is that we want to avoid controversy, whether it is with our loved ones, our spouses, our congregations, or our friends. This is where we must draw the line. We can choose to have all things appear good and not follow God, and because of the fear of controversy, watch others run the race and finish their course, without participating.

Would you rather live long and have the acceptance of men, but never achieve your purpose in life? Or would you rather live and accept controversy like Jesus, Moses, or David, and achieve your purpose in life? With controversy, they ran the race and they fulfilled their course. We must employ all courage necessary to make choices today that will determine our placement in this prophetic dispensation and in eternity before God.

I have faced many controversies for my willingness to make changes and transitions, as a result of season shiftings in the Spirit, in order to be in compliance with God's prophetic mandate for my life. It will cost you something. You must die in order to live. Paul said, *I conferred not with flesh and blood*. Friend, in order to live you must be willing to die to all that you are familiar with.

Jesus said in John 10:27, *My sheep hear my voice, and I know them, and they follow me.* Friend, have you heard the voice of God because He knows you? There are many voices out there, but stay with the Master's voice and follow not another. The reason for hearing His voice is for following, so follow His voice.

This book will challenge you to do just that. It will motivate you, it will cause stirring in your heart, and it will confront things that have never been confronted before. It will cause you to discover the needed answers to your present placement in leadership, for geographical location, for emphasis, and for new assignments.

In conclusion, the revelation in this book will empower you to run as you have never run before, see as you have never seen before, hear as you have never heard before, and give expression to the revelations of God within you that you have never given expression to before. Fight the good fight and finish your course!

Bishop Nicholas Duncan-Williams
Presiding Bishop,
ACTION CHURCHES WORLDWIDE
Founder & President,
PRAYER SUMMIT INTERNATIONAL

Chapter 1
The Transition

As I travel around the world ministering in the area of the restoration of apostolic ministry, I am finding many leaders desiring to transition from a pastoral calling to an apostolic calling. They are realizing that they have a greater calling than just being a pastor of a church. They know they need to make a transition, but do not know the steps they need to take to do it successfully.

This book is written to help leaders make the *transition*. It will provide wisdom to help churches transition from being pastoral to becoming apostolic. Our experience in Crusaders Church of Chicago helps me to help others in making the transition. We have seen our church make this transition with tremendous results.

We are currently seeing another reformation in the church. We are also experiencing *restoration*. God is restoring the ministries of apostle and prophet within the local church. As a result of this restoration, we need to reform and change the way we build churches. Unfortunately, tradition has robbed much of the Church from receiving and believing in apostles. The three ministries most churches receive and believe in are the pastor, teacher, and evangelist. Most of the leaders in the local church accept the title and function of "pastor" when it comes to starting and overseeing churches.

Most churches have been built around the pastoral anointing. The pastoral anointing has been the dominant anointing of the local church.

Most leaders have been trained to think pastorally. Bible schools and seminaries train leaders to be pastors and administrators. This is because many bible schools are staffed by former pastors, teachers, and administrators. Leaders therefore generally operate with a pastoral mind-set. Our churches have been built to meet the needs of the members, and most members expect it to remain this way. It is not uncommon to see a leader serve as a pastor of a church for many years. We commend the many pastors who have faithfully served in local churches for many years.

There is, however, a shift taking place throughout the earth. Many leaders are sensing an apostolic call. Many of them are presently pastors of local works. They are sensing and responding to a higher calling. Many have been operating in a pastoral context for so long, that they do not know how to make the transition.

This book is designed to help leaders shift into the prevailing position that God is establishing upon the earth. This prevailing position is apostolic. **Not only must leaders shift, but entire congregations must also shift.** If leaders shift without their congregations shifting, they will leave the membership behind and the result will be a gap between the leaders and the members. If leaders do not shift, the congregations will not be able to shift. If both leadership and congregations shift, you will see a quantum leap in anointing and power.

When the leadership of the church shifts, the entire church will shift as well. Our desire should be to raise up an apostolic company of believers who all have a sense of being "sent." The entire Church needs to shift into this dimension. The church in the book of Acts was first and foremost an *apostolic church.* They ministered in apostolic power and turned the known world upside down. The book is called, *The Acts of the Apostles*.

This Book will help pastors place themselves and their churches into a position to shift. It will give them the characteristics and ingredients of an apostolic ministry, including the steps they need to take to strengthen the local work. When a leader shifts into an apostolic position, the demands upon this anointing will increase substantially.

As mentioned earlier, we are now living in a time of restoration. God is restoring the apostolic ministry. He is also restoring the revelation of this ministry. Many leaders who have been called into this ministry are seeing for the first time who they really are. They are no longer looking at themselves through the eyes of tradition. There is a *shift in leadership* taking place throughout the earth. Many leaders are hearing the call to shift and transition from being pastoral to becoming apostolic. There are many leaders that are apostles, but they are so bound by the tradition of being pastors, that they do not know or see it.

You cannot fulfill an apostolic calling with a pastoral mind-set. A pastoral mind-set will limit a leader and confine him to the local church. Many leaders are beginning to realize that what they have been doing is apostolic, yet they have been limited by a pastoral mentality. They are now being challenged to fully embrace and walk in an apostolic call. I pray this book will open the eyes of many to their true calling, and they will respond and begin to walk in it.

Transition is defined as movement, passage, or change from one position, state, or stage to another. It is a period during which such changes take place. Apostolic times are seasons of transition. Change is difficult for leaders who are comfortable with the status quo. Change requires commitment and humility. It also requires listening to the voice of God and following His leading.

To "shift" means to transfer from one place, position, or person to another. It means to put aside and be replaced by another. The greatest transition and shift in the Bible occurred between the Old and New Testaments. Jesus came to bring a shift between Old Testament Judaism and the New Testament (Christian) Church. Many were not ready for the shift. Many fought against it. Those who shifted were blessed. Those who did not missed the blessing.

Leaders cannot afford to be ignorant of this restoration move of the Holy Spirit. Leaders must come into the knowledge of this current shift in the Church. There is an apostolic mandate for many senior pastors. Unless these leaders come into the knowledge of this change, many will remain locked in a pastoral mode the rest of their lives. This will drain them of their joy, zeal, and vitality. Many are already sensing this and know that they must change in order to keep their enthusiasm for ministry.

Local churches must release these leaders to function in an apostolic call. Many leaders cannot move fully into the ministry God has for them because the leadership structure is not in place for them to be released. Many of these leaders are not free to move out into a larger ministry because of the restraint placed upon them through tradition. If an apostolic leader cannot leave the church, for even a short period of time, then something is wrong. We should not build churches to depend upon one leader.

If leaders do not move into new positions, they will die spiritually within the four walls of the church. They will experience dryness, and their ministries will become routine. They will be unhappy and unsatisfied, even though it may look successful on the outside. On the inside, these ministers will feel empty. Many are afraid to transition because they think the church is dependent upon them.

Many have built their churches to depend upon them and have found satisfaction in feeling indispensable. Now they are locked into a pastoral mode and unable to move out, even though the Holy Spirit is leading them to do so. Many are afraid to leave their churches for any period of time and operate in a call to the larger body of Christ.

If most leaders would leave their churches for any period of time to do apostolic ministry, their churches would fall apart. This is not to imply that an apostle must give up a local work completely. It simply means that you must be able to obey God without losing what you have spent years building. You must build your ministry in such a way that you are not tied down, but are free to obey God.

If churches to not release their leaders to move into a higher level of ministry, they will frustrate the leaders and grieve the Holy Spirit. Churches must be set free from what they think their leaders should be and do. We will see more leaders raised up who will not fit the traditional concept of "pastor." They cannot be locked into a position and place because of the expectations and demands of the people. Both leaders and churches must be free to operate in the higher callings and gifts of God.

Leaders cannot be afraid to make this shift. Fear will paralyze you and prevent you from possessing your inheritance. There are many leaders who are even afraid of the term "apostle." They are comfortable with "pastor" because it is accepted and respected by most of the church and the community. We cannot be afraid of the terms God has given us in His word. We have received Holy Ghost inspired words to understand spiritual things (1 Corinthians 2:13).

We are living in another time of great shifting. God is realigning and restructuring the Church. After years of building churches one way, we are all of a sudden confronted with a new and better way. In order for churches to shift, there must be a shift in leadership. The leaders of the church must make the shift into a new order of ministry. This is a *paradigm shift*. A paradigm is an example serving as a model. The model for building churches is changing.

Even the world knows the importance of shifting. Economies must shift to continue to grow. We have shifted from the industrial age to the communication age. Nations and economies that do not shift are left behind and become obsolete. Obsolescence is a terrible price to pay for not being willing to change. Obsolete means to be of a discarded or an outmoded type. It means to be out-of-date.

Methods can become obsolete. Models and structures can become obsolete. Organizations can become obsolete. When something becomes obsolete it is no longer relevant. We are living in a world of change. The Church will not become obsolete in a changing world. God will upgrade our methods, structure, and models to be able to impact our world.

This change for many may seem like a quantum jump. This is a sudden and significant change, advance, or increase. The shift from a pastoral to an apostolic role is a significant jump. However, by the grace of God we can make the transition. Quantum jumps have happened throughout the history of the Church. God often moves us into greater levels of ministry quickly and suddenly. These shifts are happening quickly around the world. God has been preparing the Church for this jump. It is now time to take the leap and move into another level of anointing and power.

Challenging Tradition

In order to move into this new position, we are challenging some of the traditional ways we have been taught. Restoration will always challenge our theology and adjust our way of thinking. The New Testament pattern of planting and building churches is being restored. In the book of Acts, churches were planted by **apostles** and **apostolic teams**, *not* pastors. There is not one place in the New Testament that shows a church being planted by a **pastor**. The planting and building of churches is an **apostolic function**, not a pastoral one. It takes a **pioneering** anointing to plant churches. There is a grace upon apostles and apostolic teams to pioneer and break through. Because much of the Church does not believe in present-day apostles, many leaders who perform apostolic work have been identified as pastors. This is the title we place upon the leader of most local churches.

Because of this restoration of the ministry of apostle, we must redefine the role and function of the pastor. With *restoration* comes *reformation*. This will be painful for many who resist change and cannot see any other way of doing ministry. We must challenge the concept of a church having only one pastor. There can be many people with pastoral callings within a congregation. As churches grow and disciples multiply, there is a need for many pastors to help shepherd the flock. Pastors are not mentioned among the three governmental offices of the Church (1 Corinthians 12:28). Yet, we have made the office of pastor the governmental office of the Church.

God has set in the church, first apostles, secondarily prophets, thirdly teachers . . .
1 Corinthians 12:28

Apostles, prophets, and teachers are the governmental gifts of the church. These anointings have been left out of the government of most local churches and have been replaced by the office of pastor. This is unscriptural and grieves the Holy Spirit. We have violated God's order and have suffered for it. The result is that we have many pastors trying to build and plant churches that require an apostolic anointing, and they do not have the necessary grace to succeed. The result is many small, weak churches that cannot properly manifest the power of the kingdom of God.

On the other hand, we have seen many leaders identified as "pastors" who have planted and built strong churches, which are apostolic functions. We have locked many of them into a pastoral role and not allowed them to function in the calling of an apostle. The Church has been pastoral for so long until we have not known any other way. But God is challenging the church to change and come in line with his purpose. Once apostles are released, we will see the release of thousands of pastors within the local church to help shepherd the flock.

The cell group movement illustrates this point. The need for cell groups was birthed out of the need for believers to receive and be a part of ministry in a small group context. We have called these leaders "cell leaders" or "care leaders," when in reality they are doing the work of a pastor. They are watching over a small group. Our tradition has not allowed them to be called "pastors" because that title is reserved for the leader of the local church. It is possible to release thousands of pastors in this way. These are people gifted with a genuine call to shepherd the sheep. They have a grace to touch the flock and minister to them in a unique way. They counsel, love, heal, reach out, protect, and rescue the sheep. This should not be limited to one person or a pastoral staff of a few. God does not give associate pastors or assistant pastors, but **pastors** (Ephesians 4:11).

In Crusaders Church, we have ordained and released pastors that have caring gifts to minister to the flock. They are not in the governing presbytery of the church. They understand their pastoral gifts in relationship to the apostolic covering of the church. They are submitted to the vision of the church and do not try to form their own flock. They are shepherds within the flock. They are free to minister to the flock and are not burdened with administrative and financial duties that most pastors are concerned with. They are not bound by the traditional concept of the pastor. They do not have to be the head of the local church to function as pastors. They can fulfill their God-given duty of shepherding the sheep. They have been set free from tradition to bless the people. Churches must expand their pastoral base by acknowledging and releasing those with the gift of pastor.

Many pastors will be afraid to recognize and release other pastoral gifts for fear of them gathering small flocks around them. They have inherited a system that creates suspicion and distrust. This is why leaders must develop an apostolic mind-set. Apostles are also shepherds. When Jesus saw the multitudes as sheep without a shepherd, He sent out twelve apostles, not twelve pastors (Matthew 9:36; 10:42). Apostles have the ability to shepherd multitudes. They will have more of a rancher style of leadership. They will embrace and release pastors to help shepherd the flock, because they understand the need for them to be able to shepherd large numbers of people who are being harvested. They are not fearful and intimidated by other anointings. They are secure in their gifting, and their authority is respected by others.

In addition to pastors, churches should also have prophets (1 Corinthians 14:29). Our concept of having one pastor over a church has severely limited the other gifts from being released. This pyramid style of church government often shuts out the other gifts from fully functioning. This is especially true in the case of prophets. There are many people sitting in our churches with prophetic gifts. Leaders who have a pastoral mentality will often be afraid to release prophets. The pastoral gifting is not anointed to release gifts like the apostle's anointing. This is why our churches must become more apostolic. The pastoral anointing is also needed, but it cannot be the dominant anointing. The apostolic anointing must become the dominant anointing. It is placed in the church *first* by God. The apostle has a grace to release other gifts. As our churches migrate toward an apostolic mentality, we will see the release of many gifts—including the prophets.

The pastor thinks in terms of safety and protection. The apostle thinks in terms of expansion and progression. This does not make one better than the other. They are both needed in the church. The problem occurs when the pastoral anointing becomes the dominant anointing of the local church. The church then thinks only in terms of safety and protection, and often eliminates the other gifts that may be more radical and progressive. The result is the church becoming too pastoral at the expense of not being apostolic and prophetic. On the other hand, churches that are apostolic can be so without the expense of losing the pastoral. The apostolic ministry has the capacity to embrace the other gifts. The apostolic mentality is anointed by God to think largely and to incorporate all the gifts of God. The pastoral mind is not anointed in the same way.

This is why leaders need to embrace an apostolic mentality and dimension if they are to have the capacity to embrace and walk in all that God is releasing. Staying in a pastoral mode will hinder them from partaking fully in what is being made available during this season of restoration. Making the transition will not eliminate the pastoral anointing in the local church. On the contrary, it will release it more by releasing others to function in their pastoral gifts.

The word *first* in reference to apostles in First Corinthians 12:28 is the Greek word *proton,* meaning first in time, order, or rank. First also means principle or primary. The apostolic anointing should be the primary, foundational anointing of the Church. We are first and foremost *sent* by the risen Lord. As sent ones, we have a purpose and mission. The commission Jesus gave the church is an apostolic commission. This is why the apostolic anointing should be the dominant anointing of the Church.

The word proton is also the root of the word *prototype.* We need to see prototype churches built that will be models for the 21st century. These churches will have strong apostolic leadership. They will also have strong prophetic, teaching, pastoral, and evangelistic gifts. They will be fully functional churches. They will come behind in no gift (1 Corinthians 1:7). This will result from leaders making the necessary shift and transition into apostolic ministry. This will position the Church to receive the new wine that God is pouring into the new wineskins that are being created around the world. This will happen once the Church recognizes and walks in God's divine order of ministry for the Church.

Chapter 2
Building Antioch Churches

Now there were in the church that was at Antioch certain prophets and teachers.

Acts 13:1

The Antioch church is the model apostolic church in the Book of Acts. It is a sending church and gives us the pattern of strong presbyteries and apostolic teams. The apostolic revolves around the concept of sending and being sent. From Antioch, the team of Barnabas and Paul (and later Silas and Paul) was released for an apostolic work throughout the known world. Antioch became an apostolic mission base that affected nations and planted strategic churches. It is our prototype church that models for us an effective base that serves to establish the Kingdom of God in regions beyond.

The account of the release of the first apostolic team is found in Acts 13. As certain prophets and teachers ministered to the Lord and fasted, the Holy Ghost instructed them to release Barnabas and Paul. This apostolic team was birthed and released out of an atmosphere of the prophetic and teaching gifts. These are two of the areas that need to be strengthened in the local church in order to transition into a strong apostolic position.

Let us begin with the teaching element. If a church is to transition into an apostolic position, the minds of the people must be renewed. People must receive a revelation of the present plans and purposes of God. Apostles and prophets have a unique anointing to reveal to the Church the mysteries of God. They are stewards of the mysteries of God (1 Corinthians 4:1). They help reveal to the Church the mysteries that were hidden in previous ages (Ephesians 3:5). Once people understand the plans and purposes of the Lord, they will be able to walk in them. People need to understand what apostolic ministry is and how it relates to what the Lord is presently doing in the Church.

This is called *re-laying apostolic foundations.* The previous foundation of the Church will not be sufficient to build and expand upon. A new foundation of truth must be laid in the Church. A foundation based on present truth must be put into believers. When Paul visited Ephesus, he had to lay a new foundation within the believers. The previous foundation laid by Apollos was insufficient (Acts 19). Apollos' revelation was not sufficient, knowing only the baptism of John. This is the case with many existing churches. The present foundation is insufficient to build what the Lord is revealing today.

For years in our local church in Chicago, we have taught on the subject of apostolic ministry. The more we taught, the more revelation the Lord granted us.

. . . and unto you that hear shall more be given.

Mark 4:24

We were faithful to teach what we knew in the beginning, and God granted us more understanding as we continued to teach.

At the time, there were not many books on the subject of apostles and apostolic ministry. Most believed and taught that this ministry was not for the present-day Church. Now we have more material available than ever before. Jonathan David's book, *Apostolic Strategies Affecting Nations,* is a must to read and study. David Cannastraci's book, *Apostles and the Emerging Apostolic Movement,* and Roger Sapp's book, *The Last Apostles on Earth,* are also invaluable resource tools for today's Church. I have written several books on this subject, including *Moving in the Apostolic, The Ministry Anointing of the Apostle, Fifty Truths Concerning Apostolic Ministry, The Apostolic Church, Presbyteries and Apostolic Teams,* and *Apostolic Ministry (a 50 Lesson Bible Course).* I highly recommend that leaders read these books and begin to teach the truths to their congregations.

One reason that teaching is so important is that people will not be able to make the shift unless they shift their minds. Most people have been trained to think pastorally. They have a parish mentality. They join a church and spend all of their time and energy maintaining the church and getting their needs met. All the resources for most local churches, both natural and spiritual, go into maintaining the local church and meeting the needs of the members. People come each Sunday to hear preaching and teaching and receive healing and encouragement. The pastor is expected to preach, counsel, marry, bury, and oversee the administration of the church. This is the way most believers have been trained, and this is their understanding of the church.

The apostolic mentality is quite different. The leader is released by the people into an apostolic function to the larger Body of Christ and to geographical regions outside of the local church. The local church takes on the burden of apostolic ministry to regions beyond and to the nations. The people realize that the church is about more than just having their needs met, and that it is also about touching others with the resources that God has given us by His grace. More ministries are released to meet this burden and fulfill this vision. The church does not revolve around the ministry of one leader, but around a team of leaders with apostolic vision that comes from a revelation of proper church government. The vision to plant churches and send out teams is birthed in the heart of the people by seeing this pattern in the word of God.

In an apostolic church, the governing gifts of apostles, prophets, and teachers are set in place. The overseeing gifts of pastor and the outreach gifts of evangelist are released. The people learn to draw from all of these gifts and not depend upon the senior pastor for everything. The minds of the people must be renewed to accept and receive this order of ministry. They must be taught that this is God's order, and much of what the Church has inherited was based on tradition more than revelation.

What we are seeing is a radical change in our whole concept of the Church. Reformation always requires new teaching and restructuring of thought patterns. The people will not be able to handle such change as long as they are bound to old thought patterns. The leader must spend time teaching and training the people in new truth so that the entire church can transition into a new position.

Teaching helps release the apostolic. Teaching gives us a foundation to build upon. Whatever we do must be based upon the Word. Once people are convinced that what we are doing is scriptural, they can confidently embrace what we are building. Teaching helps us to make the necessary adjustments and corrections needed to build accurately. Teaching exposes the false concepts and foundations that we have built upon in the past.

Teaching causes us to operate in truth. Truth sets us free. A new liberty will come in releasing the church to obey the will of God. Teaching also fortifies us against the attacks of darkness that will come for obeying the truth. Once people know that what they are walking in is truth, they will not compromise because of persecution. There can be no doubt in the minds of the people that the changes are scriptural. They must be convinced that this is of God.

The people must also see the benefits of change. People will not change if there is no benefit. Why go through all the difficulty of changing if there is no benefit? They need to see the blessing of changing into an apostolic church. They must see the greater blessings and power that will flow through their church as a result of change. Reformation always causes the blessings of God to be released in a greater way. Without reformation, the Church becomes stagnant and eventually loses the full blessing of God. Through reformation, multitudes are blessed and released into their individual destinies. The Church also begins to walk in corporate destiny and release salvation and blessing to multitudes.

Transition is sometimes difficult because it requires humility and a willingness to make sacrifices. There will be a grace given by the Lord to make the change.

No man also having drunk old wine straightway desireth new: for he saith, The old is better.

Luke 5:39

People must develop an appetite for new wine. Teaching helps them develop a taste for the new wine. Once people hear about the restoration of apostles and the function of apostolic ministry, they will begin to develop a taste and appetite for it. The diet of the church must change. They cannot continue to hear the same messages of the past and be expected to change. They must receive present truth and an understanding of current moves.

I also encourage leaders to recommend books for their leadership and members to read. There is no substitute for study. Make the books available for the people. Allow them to read and study in their time away from the services. You will not be able to do it all in a Sunday morning service or a weekday Bible study. There is too much to learn in a short period of time. Give the people the resources they need to make the transition.

In addition to this, there is no substitute for bringing in an apostolic team. I cover the importance of bringing in apostolic teams in my book *Presbyteries and Apostolic Teams.* Apostolic teams help upgrade the revelation of the local church. Apostles and prophets help bring a revelation of the current moves of God. Leaders often need outside help to move the people into a new position. Revelation is a spirit, and those who have revelation can impart it to the church. The people will see and understand things through the teaching of anointed vessels. Those who have already experienced this transition and are currently walking in these truths can impart them to the church. What it took these vessels years to move into, they will impart in a short period of time to those who desire the impartation.

An *apostolic team* is a group of fivefold ministers (led by an apostle) that can come into a region or a church and build apostolically. The team comes to add to the church. They do not come to duplicate what the local leadership has already done. They help the church break through into new realms of spiritual power and revelation. We define *building apostolically* as the grace and ability to root out, pull down, destroy, throw down, build and plant (Jeremiah 1:10). Apostles and apostolic teams have the authority to pull down and build up. They pull down the strongholds of darkness and build up the saints. When a team comes into a region, there will be breakthroughs and impartations released that will add momentum to the work.

There are conferences being held throughout the world emphasizing the restoration of the apostolic ministry. I am not referring to those who are just using the terminology, but those who gather with a genuine revelation along with a desire to learn more and facilitate this move around the world. I commend the efforts of Dr. C. Peter and Doris Wagner for their desire to see this truth established in the Church. Their conferences are helping and exposing many to true restoration of apostolic ministry. Gatherings of apostles and prophets help us to meet and relate to others who are of similar spirit and faith. This strengthens leaders and helps them to continue without feeling lonely or isolated. I believe that day is coming when you will see these kinds of gatherings in every nation. God is challenging leaders in every nation to make this transition, and He is making the way for them to meet and relate to others of like faith.

Establishing the Prophetic Ministry

The other element found in the church at Antioch was the *prophetic* ministry. It was a combination of the teaching and prophetic ministries that helped birth the apostolic ministry. Local churches need to release and facilitate the prophetic ministry. The prophetic ministry should be a normal part of the ministry of the local church (1 Corinthians 14:29-32).

Many apostolic leaders will be trained in a teaching or prophetic ministry before operating fully in an apostolic calling. There is a certain maturity needed to operate as an apostle. Barnabas and Paul are identified among the prophets and teachers before they were launched into their apostolic ministries. The calling to apostleship may be present, but the release comes after a season of preparation. Apostles need to be able to operate in strong prophetic and teaching ministries. If churches develop and strengthen these ministries, they will see a greater release of the apostolic.

This is not to imply that everyone who teaches or prophesies will become an apostle. *The calling of an apostle is sovereign and based upon the will of God.* There are people who are called to be teachers and prophets. They can have an apostolic spirit, but their primary calling will be as a prophet or a teacher.

Apostolic churches need to be places of strong teaching and strong prophetic ministry. There are many teaching centers that lack strong prophetic ministry. Many of them also lack a strong apostolic presence. If the dominant anointing of the church is teaching, the other gifts may be choked out. The teaching ministry is mentioned **third** in 1 Corinthians 12:28. To make it the dominating anointing of the local church is to be out of divine order. The problem becomes emphasizing teaching at the expense of the other ministry gifts. It is similar to the discussion we had previously concerning the pastor's anointing. This can happen when the senior pastor of the local church stays in a teaching mode and does not make the transition into an apostolic calling.

Apostles teach as well as prophesy. There is more authority in the teaching of an apostle because they will teach out of the strength of the apostolic office. Teaching must be in the Church, and teachers must be released, but teaching should not be the dominant anointing of the Church. The apostolic spirit should be the foremost and primary spirit of the Church. We should be first and foremost sent ones.

The same is true concerning the prophetic ministry. This ministry is mentioned as being **second** in the church. With the restoration of the teaching ministry in the seventies and eighties, we saw an emphasis on teaching. Many, however, did not add on the prophetic ministry when it was being restored in the eighties and early nineties. I have even heard preachers say, "We don't need prophecy, all we need is the Word!"

How can we read First Corinthians 12:28, which places prophetic ministry ahead of teachers, and undervalue the prophetic ministry? God has raised up many prophetic churches that activate and release believers to prophesy. The dominant anointing of the church, however, should not be prophetic. The prophetic ministry should be secondary to the apostolic ministry. This does not minimize the importance of the prophetic ministry. The church is in dire need of prophetic ministry. There is no substitute for the prophetic.

Nevertheless, we are now seeing the restoration of apostolic ministry. This is not to say that men have not operated in this office before today. There have always been men who operated in this ministry throughout the history of the Church. However, many churches have been robbed of this vital ministry through tradition and unbelief. With restoration, there will be a return of this ministry in its fullness and in abundance. God always restores what was lost, plus more. We are seeing many leaders rise up and accept their apostolic callings around the world. With the increase of knowledge and understanding concerning this subject, there are also a greater number of leaders embracing it.

Many of these leaders have come through the restoration of the teaching and prophetic moves. They are now being birthed through the present-day *apostolic* move. Their previous training in teaching and prophetic ministry has developed and matured them for this hour. The same is true concerning many churches. They have moved through the previous moves of restoration and are now poised for this present move. Churches need to receive the restoration of the prophetic ministry to be in a position to move apostolically.

Crusaders Church of Chicago was blessed in the nineties to relate to Christian International and the ministry of Bishop Bill Hamon. God has used Christian International to help restore the prophetic ministry in a mighty way to the worldwide Church. We began to send many of our leaders to Christian International conferences to be trained and activated in prophetic ministry. In addition to Christian International, we were blessed to relate to Pastors Buddy and Mary Crum and Life Center Church of Dunwoody, Georgia. Their Activation Workshops and Prophetic Team Workshops helped train many of our current prophetic leaders. Hundreds of our members would drive and fly to these workshops to be activated and trained in prophetic ministry. As a result, we are currently activating and training hundreds of leaders around the world to minister prophetically.

We now have hundreds of people in our church that prophesy. We also have ordained prophets and prophetic teams that travel the nations. The release of the prophetic was a key step in the development of our church. One of the leaders of our prophetic ministry has been released to function as an apostle. He travels around the world with apostolic teams to help churches activate their leaders and members to prophesy. His development for apostolic ministry came through our prophetic ministry.

There are many things that will be birthed and released through prophecy. Prophetic utterances are instrumental in establishing the will of God upon the earth. There are many things that will not be released until someone declares it prophetically. In the beginning, God spoke and there was light. Light and revelation come from anointed utterances. The prophetic word releases, activates, initiates, exhorts, comforts, and confirms.

Prophetic utterances activate and release the plans and purposes of God. The prophetic word is creative. Prophecy not only informs us of what God is doing, but it actually triggers the move (Psalm 105:31, 34). Prophecy does more than confirm, it releases. This is true concerning both personal prophecy and corporate prophecy.

Prophets carry a tremendous amount of authority. Their utterances break through the demonic opposition that is set to hinder the plans and purposes of God. Churches that have strong prophetic utterance over individuals and regions will see a greater momentum and breakthrough in establishing what is being revealed by the Holy Spirit. The prophetic will help release the apostolic. The apostolic also releases the prophetic. These two ministries complement and stir one another.

For years we have heard prophetic words concerning the direction of our local church.

Prophecies concerning our apostolic call were heard continually. We heard these things before we began to experience much of what we are walking in today. For years I received prophecies concerning an apostolic call. These words helped to encourage me to pursue and believe in the call. Apostolic leaders need the confirmation of proven prophetic ministries. This will encourage them and help to activate the gift inside.

Everything we are doing today was declared prophetically before we did it. Prophecy thrusts you into the purposes of God. It encourages you to move into the will of God. It releases faith to operate beyond what you are accustomed to. It helps to break the barriers and limitations we have accepted through tradition or lack of knowledge. I cannot overemphasize the importance of teaching on and releasing the prophetic ministry within the local church. This is instrumental in helping a church move fully into an apostolic ministry.

When we speak of prophetic ministry, we are not limiting it to prophets. We are also including prophecy as one of the gifts of the Holy Spirit, and the *spirit of prophecy* that every believer has through the indwelling of the Holy Spirit. We make a distinction between the simple gift of prophecy and the ministry of the prophet. Every believer can prophesy (Acts 2:16-18). Prophesy is utterance that comes from being filled with the Spirit (Acts 19:6). We know that everyone is not a prophet

(1 Corinthians 12:29). Prophets prophesy with more authority and revelation because they speak from the strength and position of their office. The simple gift of prophecy, however, is speaking unto men to edification, exhortation, and comfort (1 Corinthians 14:3).

Prophecy is a building gift. To *edify* means to build. We get our word *edifice* from this word, which means a building or a structure. Prophecy is an integral part of building the Church. When we build people, we build the Church. Prophecy will strengthen believers, giving them the necessary strength to move into apostolic ministry. It strengthens and builds the spirits of the people. People with strong spirits will be able to transition and move into the fullness of what the Lord is releasing.

I cannot overemphasize the importance of prophecy. Churches should excel in it (1 Corinthians 14:12). To *excel* means to do extremely well. Our prophetic level should not be mediocre. We should not be average or sub-par in this area. People need to be activated and trained to flow in the spirit of prophecy. We need to take time to teach in this area and make room for its operation. It will not happen by accident. We must have a strategy to raise the level of the prophetic ministry in the local church.

Chapter 3
A New Order for a New Move

But new wine must be put into new bottles; and both are preserved.

Luke 5:38

And it came to pass in those days, that he went out into a mountain to pray, and continued all night in prayer to God.

And when it was day, he called unto him his disciples: and of them he chose twelve, whom also he named apostles;

Simon, (whom he also named Peter,) and Andrew his brother, James and John, Philip and Bartholomew,

Matthew and Thomas, James the son of Alpheus, and Simon called Zealots,

And Judas, the brother of James, and Judas Iscariot, which also was the traitor.

Luke 6:12-16

Why did Jesus choose twelve apostles? Why didn't he choose twelve prophets or priests? Jesus ordained and released a new order of ministry. The ministry of apostle is a New Testament ministry. Although Moses, Samuel, and David are Old Testament types of the apostle, they are identified as prophets. Jesus was establishing a new order of ministry before the outpouring of the Holy Spirit on the Day of Pentecost. The Old Testament wineskin of Judaism with priests, prophets, judges, and kings could not handle the new wine of the Holy Spirit. The New Testament wineskin of the Church, with the presence of apostles, is needed to contain the new wine.

Joel's prophecy emphasizes prophecy as an element of the last day outpouring. The sons and daughters will prophesy. The servants and handmaidens will prophesy. The young men shall see visions and the old men dream dreams. This is a radical release of all people. It makes no difference whether you are male or female, young or old, rich or poor, all can prophesy and operate in a prophetic realm. In the Old Testament, only a select group were anointed to minister. The old wineskin of Judaism could not contain such a release of anointing. **The Holy Spirit releases all believers into ministry.**

Every reformation has brought about a release of all believers. The Protestant reformation in the 16th Century emphasized the priesthood of all believers. The Asuza revival of the 20th Century emphasized the Holy Spirit baptism and speaking in tongues for all believers. We have also learned that all believers can cast out devils, heal the sick, and do the works of Jesus (John 14:12). These things are no longer relegated to the clergy. Now we are seeing a release of all believers flowing prophetically and apostolically. This does not make all apostles and prophets, but all believers can operate in these dimensions.

God has raised up apostolic leaders to release believers throughout the history of the Church. This is what the apostolic anointing is equipped to do. It takes an apostolic grace to be able to facilitate such releases. It has always been a radical concept to release the majority. Most religious leaders are afraid to do so. They are afraid they will lose control. Apostles help create new wineskins. Old wineskins cannot handle this kind of expansion.

Old wineskins are rigid and inflexible. Organizations and churches often become legalistic and dogmatic. It is their way or no way. When this happens, God raises up apostolic and prophetic leadership, which brings a fresh word and help to create new wineskins. These anointings are more radical and progressive. They attract a new group of believers who are not held back and bound by a religious mind-set. The result is the formation of new wineskins.

Apostolic leaders will often be branded as troublemakers and heretics. Martin Luther was not the favorite preacher of many in his day. His preaching and teaching was radical. He put the Word of God into the hands of the common people. This broke the stranglehold of the privileged few. He upset the status quo. He dared to challenge the concept of clergy over laity.

The new wineskin comes into being when men rediscover truth. It has been there all the time, but hidden by the tradition of the Church. The spirit of revelation comes to open the eyes of believers to the truth. This truth is preached in spite of opposition. What was birthed in the heat of reformation becomes standard truth in the years to come.

In order to transition successfully, a new wineskin must be developed. Leadership must concentrate on developing this new wineskin. The structure and format of the church must change. One cannot be afraid to change the structure of the church in order to create a new wineskin. The models of the past will not be sufficient to handle what God is doing today. We must receive the new blueprints that the Holy Spirit is giving us. Apostles are wise master builders (1 Corinthians 3:10). They are spiritual architects. They build by revelation, not tradition.

Many of the models that leaders used to build are outmoded and outdated. We must upgrade our technologies and build according to the current patterns being released from heaven. The blueprints are here. We need to embrace them and believe they provide a structure that will cause a greater degree of blessing and glory to be released. You cannot put the new wine into old wineskins. The wineskins must change. There is no way to get around this truth.

This is why apostles must be in place. The ministry of apostle is the new order of ministry for the outpouring of the new wine. Apostolic churches are new wineskins. The apostolic anointing is the only anointing capable of overseeing and releasing all believers into the fullness of what the Holy Spirit is releasing.

Most churches governed by a pastoral mentality have not been able to release the gifts of God fully. Many pastors are afraid to release prophesy, deliverance, and other supernatural ministries for fear of losing control. These things cannot be administrated and organized in the flesh. Many pastors think in terms of maintaining order and safety within the local church. The apostolic and prophetic gifts are more radical and progressive. Apostles are pioneers and risk takers. They are not afraid to receive and release new things.

As long as our churches are governed by pastoral mind-sets, you will continue to see many gifts restricted and held back. There are many people with apostolic and prophetic gifts who are frustrated in churches because of leaders who are unable to release them. Many of these leaders have good hearts, but they lack the apostolic grace to facilitate what the Lord desires to do. There are also leaders with apostolic callings who cannot fully activate and release the people because they have been trained to think and operate pastorally. The pastoral mind-set has hindered many that have higher callings. Many leaders have been trained in Bible schools and seminaries to think pastorally and administratively. How many schools can one attend today that teach and train people to operate apostolically and prophetically?

The apostolic ministry has been set in the Church to oversee and release all believers into their callings and destinies. The apostle's mind-set is conducive to accomplish this. The apostle should not think only in terms of maintaining, but also in terms and areas of expanding. There is room for all of the gifts to operate in an apostolic church. This ministry provides a framework large enough to house all God desires to do. There is a capacity to contain the new wine without breakage and spillage. There is no limit to the numbers of ministries released when the leaders embrace and walk in an apostolic call.

Not only did Jesus choose and ordain twelve apostles, He identified them. How does this apply to use today? The lord is calling apostles forth around the world and identifying them. We are going to know who they are. He is calling them out of obscurity. They will no longer be hidden from the eyes of the Church. We need to know the signs of a true apostle to test those who claim apostleship. Once they are identified, we can receive and benefit from their ministries.

Many of these leaders will be identified by their response to the truth. Their spirits will leap when they hear the message. There will be an excitement that comes. Their spirits will be charged, and they will have a hunger to know more. We are seeing this happen all over the world. The response has been overwhelming. It has been surprising to see how many leaders have been in preparation for this day.

Many of these leaders will also be identified prophetically. They will receive the independent confirmation of proven prophetic ministries. I received a prophecy concerning apostolic ministry in 1989. At that time, I knew nothing about the ministry of the apostle. I had to pursue this ministry by faith. God has led me for these many years by His grace. Since then, I have received many confirming prophetic words. John the Baptist identified Jesus as the Lamb of God (John 1:29-34). Ananias identified Paul as a chosen vessel (Acts 9:10-16).

Many can be identified by their works. Jesus pointed to His works to show He was a sent one (John 5:36). The work will speak for itself. There are many leaders that are presently doing apostolic work around the world. There are many who have not yet done the work, but the calling is there. They can draw alongside of a proven apostolic ministry to be trained and matured. The twelve were identified as apostles before they ever planted a church. They were sent out by Jesus to preach, heal, cast out devils, and raise the dead. They would not have qualified for this ministry in the eyes of many today. They had no seminary training or divinity degrees. They were simply chosen, trained, and sent.

Some would say, "It is not important to be called an apostle, just do the work." I agree that it is better to have the work without the title, than the title without the work. There are many who would claim apostleship without having the signs of a proven apostolic ministry. We are to test those who claim apostleship (Revelation 2:2). It is, however, important for people to know their gift and calling in order to be able to walk in it confidently and boldly. Jesus knew that He was sent. Paul identified himself as an apostle by the will of God. He even defended his apostleship.

When people do not know their identity, they will often miss their purpose. The devil tries to keep people from knowing who they are. He blinds the minds of many to keep them from their true identity. A person who knows who he is becomes a threat to the kingdom of darkness. Gideon did not know he was a mighty man of valor. Moses did not know he was the deliverer of Israel. They had to come into their identities to bring deliverance to Israel.

Identity is defined as the condition of being oneself, and not another. What a powerful thought! When you know your identity, you can be yourself!

You don't have to try to be what you are not. David could not wear Saul's armor. He was not comfortable trying to be what he was not. He used the weapons that were comfortable for him, and he killed Goliath. There are too many leaders trying to be what religion and tradition says they should be. They are trying to fit in a mold that they are not created for.

The apostolic leaders that are coming forth will not be identified by their association to a particular group or denomination. Paul was not a part of the twelve. His call to apostleship was not based on their approval or knowledge. When he finally met James, Peter, and John, they recognized his apostolic call and extended to him the right hand of fellowship (Galatians 2:7-9). We cannot limit this ministry to our group or denomination. God chooses and calls whom He desires.

Those identified will take their place in the new order of ministry established by our Lord two thousand years ago. This ministry is one of the benefits of the New Testament. They have a better covenant based upon better promises. All shall know the Lord, from the least to the greatest (Hebrews 8:8-12). This new covenant ministry, along with the other New Testament gifts, are for the perfecting of the saints. The saints will be matured to do the work of the ministry. The Church will receive the full blessing of the covenant established by Jesus. The next chapters will deal with areas that must be strong in the local church if both the leaders and church expect to shift into an apostolic position. We have experienced these things in our local work in Chicago. The following are characteristics and ingredients of apostolic churches and apostolic people.

Chapter 4
Prayer and Deliverance

Pray ye therefore the Lord of the harvest, that he would send forth laborers into his harvest.

Matthew 9:38

But we will give ourselves continually to prayer, and to the ministry of the word.

Acts 6:4

Prayer releases the apostolic spirit. Prayer releases **sent ones.** This is an apostolic term. Apostle means **sent one.** *Churches that want to transition into an apostolic position must have strong prayer and intercession.* The prayer base of the local church must be increased.

Prayer is also the power source of the apostolic. The apostles gave themselves continually to prayer. This is also true concerning apostolic churches. There will be a spirit of grace and supplication (Zechariah 12:10). Apostles must be free from all of the normal administrative duties placed on most church leaders. They must be free to give themselves to prayer and the ministry of the Word. Many pastors work themselves to death with counseling and administrative duties. The people have come to expect the pastor to do everything. This is what he is paid to do, some may reason, but apostles must be released to cover a wider area of ministry. They must release themselves by releasing others. This is hard for some leaders to do. They have operated so long in a pastoral and administrative role that it will be hard for them to transition.

As we began to move into an apostolic position, intercession and prayer became a key to breakthrough into stronger realms of anointing. Jesus prayed all night before choosing the twelve (Luke 4:12). All-night prayer is a key to releasing the apostolic spirit. The power released in prayer will give leaders and churches the strength they need to proceed. Corporate prayer was a characteristic of the early church (Acts 4:24). The whole church must be mobilized to prayer. Apostolic and prophetic leaders need to lead the congregation in strong praying.

Each time the Lord revealed to us new truth about the apostolic ministry, we would pray corporately concerning that truth. Whatever was preached, we would pray to be established. We prayed the prophecies that were spoken in our local church. We prayed for the grace to walk in what we were hearing. Prayer was an integral part of establishing the truth in our church.

We also bound the demon spirits in our region that were set on stopping what the Lord was saying. We prayed for angels to be released into our region to help us break through the resistance of the powers of darkness in our region. This must be done in prayer. We must war according to prophecy (1 Timothy 1:18).

Diversities of tongues (1 Corinthians 12:28) is an important gift in this area. Many prayer warriors will operate in diversities of tongues. There are great breakthroughs that will come through this gift. Utterances in other tongues will help us pray in a supernatural way, beyond the limitations of our understanding. We can pray beyond our limited understanding of what God is releasing and restoring. Those who operate in the gift of diversities of tongues can release much through the various utterances of the Spirit.

The apostolic prayers of Paul are important to open the eyes of believers and cause them to know their calling. Paul prayed that the eyes of the Church's understanding would be enlightened. He prayed for the believers to have the spirit of revelation (Ephesians 1:17-18). He prayed that they would walk worthy of the Lord unto all pleasing, being fruitful in every good work, and increasing in the knowledge of God (Colossians 1:10-11).

Apostolic churches must labor in prayer that the saints would stand perfect and complete in all the will of God (Colossians 4:12). Prayer neutralizes the powers of hell that would hinder believers from breaking through into new levels of revelation and grace.

Deliverance - Increasing the Level of Freedom in a Church

And when he had called unto him his twelve disciples, he gave them power against unclean spirits, to cast them out.

Matthew 10:1

The first thing Jesus gave the twelve before sending them forth was power over unclean spirits. Deliverance is a major part of the apostle's equipment to break through and establish the Kingdom of God. The apostolic ministry is a ministry of liberty (2 Corinthians 3:17). The people must be free to obey and walk in this ministry. This is why deliverance is a major key.

If demons are not exposed and cast out, they will hinder the purposes of God from being fulfilled. The more deliverance people receive, the freer they will be to walk in the Spirit and obey the word of God. Casting out demons breaks the power of the enemy in a region and creates an environment of freedom. There will be a greater liberty in an apostolic church to believe and operate in power and anointing.

Because so many people need deliverance, we have no choice but to train and release multitudes of believers to cast out devils. This is the first sign that should follow a believer (Mark 16:17). Every believer needs to be mobilized to carry the apostolic burden of the local church. Apostolic churches are called to pull down strongholds in regions over which they have jurisdiction.

This is another reason why we must have an apostolic mentality prevailing in our churches. Deliverance is frightening to many leaders. They want to relegate it to a side room in the church, instead of making it an integral part of the church. It is not a safe ministry. Dealing with demons is too unpleasant and risky for many leaders. They would rather spend hours counseling people who have demonic problems. Many want to substitute teaching for deliverance.

Apostles, however, are sent to destroy the works of the devil. Power and authority over demons is a sign of an apostolic ministry. Casting out devils is necessary to establish the Kingdom of God (Matthew 12:18). Apostolic churches will manifest power and authority over the demons of a particular territory. This will give them the ability to penetrate and pioneer in that region..

Crusaders Church was exposed to the ministry of deliverance in 1985. At that time, we had no understanding of apostolic ministry. We did not know that what we were entering into was an apostolic function. Amid much controversy and misunderstanding, we were faithful to press into this ministry. It was laid in the foundation of our church, and it continues to be an integral part of the ministry.

Most of the members of Crusaders Church have received deliverance and have been trained to cast out devils. We taught for years in the area of deliverance, and we continue to do so. Books by Frank Hammond, Win Worley, Derek Prince, Don Basham, and other pioneers of the deliverance ministry helped to us understand the importance of deliverance. Books written recently by Bill Subritzky, Peter Horribin, and Noel and Phyl Gibson are powerful tools to instruct believers in the area of deliverance.

There is no substitute for the ministry of Deliverance. The freedom that comes from casting out demons enables believers to rise to new levels of faith and obedience. It also opens the way for evangelism. The controlling powers of darkness are neutralized, and more people respond to the preaching of the gospel. It is a key to opening up entire regions to be evangelized. The heavens are opened and the blessings of God are released.

Deliverance is necessary to attack and drive out religious spirits that have aborted and hindered much of what God desires to do. Spirits of witchcraft and generational spirits must also be challenged and driven out. Deliverance opens the way for holiness. Cleanliness and purity must be in place to keep the Church from being diverted from its course.

Deliverance will strengthen the local church. Contending with demons and overcoming them will inspire faith and confidence. The level of discernment will also increase. Members will have their senses exercised to discern good and evil (Hebrews 5:14). This will enable them to handle the strong meat of the Word. They will become adept in spiritual warfare and will be able to handle the pressure that comes with apostolic ministry. Apostolic ministry is a tough ministry that requires fortitude and perseverance. The experience gained in casting out demons is invaluable.

One of the functions of the apostolic ministry is warfare. The word *warfare* in 2 Corinthians 10:4, is the Greek word **strateia,** which means apostolic career. The *apostolic career* is one of warfare. Deliverance helps the believers to learn warfare. God teaches our hands to war and our fingers to fight (Psalm 144:1). Apostolic churches are warring churches. They have the grace and anointing to pull down strongholds.

There are many strongholds that will not be pulled down without an apostolic anointing. Two of the outstanding characteristics of an apostolic ministry are power and authority (Matthew 10:1). There is an authority resident in the apostolic anointing to confront and pull down strongholds. These strongholds are the mind-sets that are contrary to the will of God. The rank of the apostle makes him a formidable combatant against the powers of darkness. Demons recognize and submit to this anointing.

God trains us through hand-to-hand combat with the enemy. Deliverance is often referred to as *ground-level warfare.* Apostolic churches become God's boot camp to train His army to invade and drive out the enemy. We have seen thousands of believers strengthened and trained through casting out demons. They must use their faith and gifts to deal with demons. They come to experientially know the victory of Christ over the enemy.

When believers deal with demons on a continual basis, they will mature in warfare. You will have a group of proven soldiers who will be able to contend with the powers of darkness on a higher level. The Church can then be successful in *strategic-level warfare.* This is dealing with territorial spirits that control a region or a territory. Breakthroughs in these territories are contingent upon the binding of these powers. Once these powers are bound, there will be a new liberty and openness to the gospel in that region.

Chapter 5
Developing Teams

And he ordained twelve, that they should be with him, and that he might send them forth to preach.

Mark 3:14

Jesus ordained the twelve to be a part of His team. As members of His team, they could then be sent forth. As leaders develop teams, they will be able to send the team members forth. Apostolic leaders ordain and release. This is the pattern of ministry given by our Lord. Jesus is the apostle of our profession. He is the perfect apostle. As an apostle, He released other apostles. We will see apostles that ordain and release other apostles.

If a leader is to make a successful transition from a pastoral into an apostolic role, he must develop a team of leaders that will help carry the burden of ministry. Without a strong team, the burden of ministry in the local work will fall directly upon him. The development of the team will help release the leader into an apostolic role. It will free him to move out into a greater ministry to the larger body of Christ. It is crucial to release pastors to tend to the flock. It is also important to develop a team of governmental leaders who continue to give direction and oversight to the work.

In Crusaders Church, we have seen a team of apostles, prophets, and teachers come together to guard and direct the work. The apostolic leaders are able to take teams around the world to impact nations. The prophets are released to help give direction and insight into what the Lord is directing us to do. The teachers are released to train new members and believers as well as to provide a strong Word foundation for members of the church. These governmental anointings work together as a team. The work has grown too large for one man and a few assistants to handle.

Apostolic ministry is team ministry. Jesus gathered a team around him and trained them for three and a half years. He also sent out the seventy in teams of two (Luke 10:1). The Antioch church released apostolic teams to plant churches and travel throughout the known world. The traditional concept of having one pastor and some associates to pastor the flock is being challenged. We are now developing and establishing presbyteries that will be able to govern the local church. These presbyteries will consist of apostles, prophets, and teachers which are the governing gifts of the Church (1 Corinthians 12:28). They will serve as a team that gives direction and covering for the local church.

The presbytery is able to prophesy and impart (1 Timothy 4:14). They have an apostolic mentality because they have apostolic leadership within the presbytery. The order and ranking of ministry is respected within the presbytery. From the presbytery leaders can be released for ministry outside the local church, just as at the church at Antioch. The Church becomes an apostolic resource center because of developed leaders who can be released at the leading of the Holy Spirit.

The *presbytery* is the team that oversees and gives direction to the local church. This keeps the church strong and makes it a powerful witness in the community. *Apostolic teams* are groups that are sent out to affect regions beyond the local area. Some leaders can function in both. When at home, the leaders can be part of the presbytery. When going out, they can be part of an apostolic team. Some will be set primarily in the presbytery. Some will spend more time going out as part of an apostolic team.

This concept of ministry needs to be taught to the Church. Believers must come in to agreement with it and make the necessary changes to accommodate it. The Antioch church becomes our model church. The Church begins to migrate from a pastoral position to an apostolic one without losing the pastoral dimension. The members will still be cared for because of the release of pastors. The Church will move beyond being a parish and have a greater impact in different regions and territories. This includes planting churches and building apostolically in the places where teams are sent.

A team is stronger than one man. A team of apostles, prophets, and teachers carries tremendous authority in the spirit realm. The powers of hell must recognize the authority of these teams and submit. The church needs to be able to release apostolic teams, prophetic teams, evangelistic teams, and deliverance teams to other churches and regions. This will give an apostle a greater ability to impact and influence a wider territory than he can influence by himself.

Many churches are led by a charismatic leader who may have a pastoral staff to assist him. The ministry revolves around this one leader. This is a pastoral mentality that must be changed to release other apostles, prophets, and teachers, as well as pastors and evangelists. As a leader shifts into an apostolic role, he must develop and release teams of strong ministers. He cannot be intimidated by strong gifts and anointings. The Lord will send many strong gifts to an apostle because of the grace upon this ministry to activate, train, and release gifts. They are not sent to support his ministry only, but to be instrumental in fulfilling the apostolic vision given to the church. Some will be sent out as apostles to plant churches and duplicate in other places what they have seen at the home base. Teams will be released to go to nations to extend the Kingdom of God.

The Antioch church illustrates the team concept. The church at Jerusalem sent Barnabas to help with the work (Acts 11:22). Barnabas departed to Tarsus to recruit Paul to come and help with the work. Barnabas and Paul assembled themselves at Antioch to teach for a year (Acts 11:25-26). They labored together as a team at Antioch. They were later sent out as a team from Antioch (Acts 13:1-4).

First Thessalonians chapter 2 gives us revelation concerning the apostolic team. The team exhorts, teaches, preaches, comforts, charges, and imparts. A team consists of leaders with different anointings, whose gifts complement each other. They work together and each member lends his/her strength to the whole. The devil hates and fears the work of the team. The team can break through where one person cannot.

Churches that develop presbyteries and apostolic teams will take on the burden for entire nations and regions. They will have the capacity to touch these regions because they will have teams available to be released. Their governmental structure enables them to reach out without the home base falling apart. People are their greatest resources and apostolic grace enables them to do more than the average church. They become models that can be reproduced and multiplied in other places.

Presbyteries to apostolic teams are keys to churches being able to reach out to nations.

Presbyteries provide a pool of proven ministries. From this pool, the Holy Spirit can draw and send out. The apostolic team is God's end-time strategy to affect nations. The line (measure) of the Church must extend to the uttermost parts of the earth. Our ability to reach out and touch multitudes in a personal way is proportionate to the development and release of apostolic teams.

The results of shifting from a pastoral mode to an apostolic mode will be numerous. The very nature of the church will change. This includes its emphasis and lifestyle. The members will begin to adopt an apostolic lifestyle that will change the way they think, act, and live. They will develop a team mentality. Every area of the church will be affected. This includes the preaching, teaching, prayer, worship, finances, vision, and outreach.

The messages from the pulpit will change. The content of the messages will be deeper, and will affect those who hear them in a deeper way. More revelation will come forth that will cause the believers to have an understanding of the mysteries of God. The messages will emphasize the corporate destiny the church. Revelation will change the church and cause the believers to live a lifestyle that is opposed to the individualistic way of thinking that most people live by.

The strategies of the church will change. Apostolic strategies will come forth, enabling the church to execute the plans and purposes of God.

This strategy will include teams. This is a higher way of thinking that is conducive to carrying out the commissions given to the Church. New spiritual technologies will be released that will give the Church the ability to do what could not be done previously.

The people will experience a greater degree of glory and liberty. When the dominant anointing is apostolic, the people will come into contact with a higher frequency and will become accustomed to it. They will be able to operate in higher levels of anointing, and they will live and minister in higher levels of glory.

Apostles will challenge and demand performance from the saints. Pastors have been guilty of doing the work for the people, whereas apostles demand that the people rise to a new level of maturity. The dependency upon the pastor is broken. The saints are expected to grow and perform on a higher level. The apostolic ministry raises the standard and expects more. It is not a caretaker, baby-sitting ministry.

Apostles will mobilize large groups of people for ministry. Jesus released the twelve, and then He released the seventy. They were able to duplicate His ministry of preaching, healing, and deliverance throughout Israel. He then released the disciples to go into all the world and teach all nations. The apostolic ministry is one of duplication and multiplication. The Church should not have to depend upon mission boards and Para church ministries to fulfill the Great Commission. The Church is responsible for destroying the gates of hell.

Teams make it possible for more people to exercise their gifts. When the responsibilities of ministry are shared, more people get involved. As more people come into the Kingdom, we will have no choice but to develop and release teams. The needs of humanity are too great. If we are believing for a harvest, we must prepare to meet their needs. God has released an abundance of gifts to meet the needs of the lost. We are living in a day of abundance of grace. The apostolic ministry is a ministry of great grace (Acts 4:33).

When we started our deliverance ministry, we were overwhelmed by the number of people who came for ministry. We had to quickly train hundreds of deliverance workers to minister to those needing help. The same was true concerning prophetic ministry. The response to the prophetic was overwhelming. We had to train hundreds of people to be able to minister the Word of the Lord to those who came for ministry. People respond to the supernatural. Everywhere Jesus went, He was overwhelmed by the crowds. He had to train and release a team to minister to the multitudes.

As the Church's vision expands, and it will, once a shift is made into the apostolic, the necessity to raise up teams will become obvious. God will put the multitudes in our hearts. We will carry the burden of helping the multitudes. We will develop the means to touch them. People are our greatest resources. There is no substitute for anointed people. They are the tools to get the job done.

Chapter 6
Helps and Governments

These two ministries are mentioned in 1 Corinthians 12:28 after miracles and gifts of healings. They are important to the work of the Church. The *helps ministry* needs to be strong in an apostolic church to assist the leadership in carrying out the vision. There are people anointed in the area of helps. They have the grace to assist apostles in carrying out the apostolic mandate. They have authority to help. Their authority must be recognized and released.

Early in the development of our church, we saw the need to release the ministry of helps in the church. The teachings by Buddy Bell were especially helpful. He taught that this is a supernatural ability given by God to assist. These are supportive ministries that hold up the hand of the leaders. This is typified by Aaron and Hur lifting up the hands of Moses (Exodus 17:12).

The apostles recognized the need for "helps" when they instructed the congregation to choose seven men to assist in ministering to the widows. This freed them to give themselves to prayer and the ministry of the Word (Acts 6:1-7). The result was an increase of the Word of God and a multiplication of disciples. The deacon's ministry is a helps ministry. This ministry needs to be strong in the local church. It has to be strengthened to carry the burden of the local church. Deacons and others in helps ministry need to know their strategic importance in the plan of God. Without them, an apostle will not be able to carry out the vision. Helps is a ministry. This needs to be taught and recognized by the Church.

Apostolic churches must be strong in the area of helps. This can include those who stand by and serve the apostle in a very personal way. They know what is needed and help to facilitate the directives of the apostolic leadership. We spent many years teaching in the area of helps, and continue to have a regular class in this area. When this anointing is released in a church, the apostle will be free to give himself to prayer and the ministry of the Word.

Governments, on the other hand, is the gift of administrations. There are people anointed in the area of administrations who have the gift to help organize and facilitate such a large vision. With so much released through the restoration of apostolic ministry, this anointing is a must. This person is anointed to delegate responsibilities and to direct groups of people. They have practical wisdom to help administrate what the apostolic leadership is releasing and establishing. We need to recognize this anointing as an integral part of the church.

Administration must be submitted to the governing anointings of the church. Many denominations and groups of churches have allowed the administrative anointing to become the dominant anointing of the church. Many of these groups are run by administrators. Everything revolves around organization. Every directive comes from headquarters. Many apostolic and prophetic ministries have been killed by administrators. When this anointing supersedes the apostolic anointing, the church will not be able to progress into new things. Apostles need organization, but they cannot be hindered or controlled by it. The organization is made for the apostle, not the apostle for the organization. Organization is meant to help us, not control us.

Administrators help us work out the practical aspects of fulfilling the vision. They think in a practical way, which is necessary to get the job done. Everything is not dreams, visions, and revelations. These things set the course, but governments help bring it into reality. They can design and implement programs that bring the apostle's vision into reality. When this anointing is submitted to the apostle's vision, it will be a blessing to the Church. When it is out of position, it will hinder the plan of God. Administrators are not anointed to lead the Church, apostles are. They can recommend to the leadership practical ways to carry out the vision.

Administrators help work the details of carrying out the vision. They deal with the small matters that are important to the overall success of the project. This takes a load off of the apostolic leaders. The apostolic leaders can then focus on the overall vision. The administrators also develop and set up the administrative arm of the church. Churches can rise or fall on the strength or weakness of administration.

Some leaders are more administrative than others. Some are more visionary. Some are both visionary and administrative. Leaders must have people with strong administrative gifts to help them. The senior leaders cannot become bogged down with too much administration. Some leaders wear themselves down with administration. They experience burnout because they do not recognize others with this gifting, and they do not know how to delegate. Some churches expect pastors to be administrators. They expect the leaders to *be* and to *do* everything.

A vision without administration is like a body without a skeleton. The skeleton holds up the body. Administrations is the bone structure of the Church. This is why administrations must be strong in the church.

Some apostolic leaders are very administrative. Axel Sippach of Seattle, Washington is an apostolic and visionary strategist with a strong gift of administration. He is also one of the apostolic leaders of our I.M.P.A.C.T. Network who has been a tremendous blessing in helping administrate much of what we are doing around the world. Apostle Sippach is gifted in strategizing the plans of God including how to move, penetrate, and establish the apostolic in certain nations.

However, he still needs those with administrative gifts to help carry out the vision. When he becomes too bogged down with administration, it draws his focus away from the overall vision he has as an apostolic leader. God gives him strategies to impact and affect nations. With the help of governments, Axel can be effective in implementing these strategies.

Chapter 7
Releasing Evangelists

Evangelists are not intended to be stuck in the government of the Church. They need to be free to minister to the lost, as the pastors are free to minister to the sheep. The Church has had less of a problem recognizing and releasing evangelists. They were not a threat to most pastors because they were a traveling ministry. The church also believed in the ministry of the evangelist as one viable for today. The apostles and prophets have not fared as well.

Evangelists will help bring in the harvest. Evangelists need to be connected to apostolic churches. Apostolic churches are structured to be able to handle and maintain the harvest that comes through evangelism. Philip the Evangelist called for the apostles to come to Samaria after seeing an evangelistic breakthrough. It is not enough to see people saved. They must be baptized in the Holy Spirit and incorporated into the Church. The apostles came to lay hands on the believers to be filled with the Holy Spirit (Acts 8). The apostles can teach, train, and impart to the new believers after the evangelist leaves.

There are many evangelists sitting in our pews who need to be released. The apostle's vision should be large enough to incorporate and release them into the vision of the church. They need to be recognized, ordained, and released. Their ministries will be more fruitful if they are recognized and released by apostles. The evangelist is also given for the perfecting of the saints. They will help release an evangelistic spirit into the church. They should also operate in an apostolic dimension by receiving the impartation available in the church. Their vision will also be apostolic. They will not be limited by the traditional concept of what it means to be an evangelist. They will operate in a higher level of revelation and power.

Philip the evangelist came out of an apostolic community in Jerusalem and saw great breakthrough in Samaria. He ministered with an apostolic spirit. He was able to go into an area controlled by witchcraft and break through. He pioneered in evangelism into a new area. We need pioneering evangelists to be a part of breaking into new regions and territories.

Apostles have the grace to release these gifts. God is the One that gives these gifts by His grace. The pastoral structure of many churches today hinders many evangelists from functioning. An apostolic vision is large enough to embrace them all. Furthermore, the apostle recognizes the need for these gifts. The vision is too large to complete without them. They should teach the church their importance and place within the church. Apostles stir evangelists through preaching and teaching, and help release them by faith. Evangelists must not draw back because of fear and tradition. They cannot wait for others, but must be willing to pioneer if necessary. They must trust in the grace of God to get the job done. Evangelists must be willing to suffer persecution and misunderstanding from religious people for the sake of establishing the truth. They must build by revelation, not tradition.

The Church for years has been taught that the Great Commission is an evangelistic commission. It is, however, an apostolic commission. The commission was given to apostles, and it will take an apostolic anointing and strategy to fulfill it. Evangelism is a key part of this strategy. Without evangelists and evangelism, we will not be able to fulfill the commission. Teams of evangelists will be needed for the Church to reach the lost. The joining of the evangelistic to the apostolic will cause a greater harvest to be reaped.

We are seeing the release of apostolic reformers. They have the grace and anointing to reform and restructure the Church according to the biblical pattern. They will have all the materials they need because of restoration. Apostolic churches will have an abundance of grace. There will be no lack. We are to come behind in no gift while waiting for the coming of the Lord (1 Corinthians 1:7).

Chapter 8
The Tabernacle of David

How shall not the ministration of the spirit be rather glorious?

2 Corinthians 3:8

Now the Lord is the Spirit: and where the Spirit of the Lord is, there is liberty.

But we all, with open face beholding as in a glass the glory of the Lord, are changed into the same image from glory to glory, even as by the Spirit of the Lord.

2 Corinthians 3:17-18

The second epistle to the Corinthians is a defense given by Paul concerning his apostolic ministry. He identified this New Testament ministry as a ministry of glory. The people are changed as they come into contact with the glory of God. The apostolic provides an atmosphere of glory for people to come and be changed.

Once the apostolic and prophetic dimensions are released in a church, the very nature of the church will change. This is especially true in the area of praise and worship. The release of anointed psalmists and minstrels will cause a greater release of God's glory in the church. An open heaven over the ministry will result in a greater liberty in praise and worship.

I encourage leaders to do a teaching on the Tabernacle of David which is being restored according to Acts 15:15-19. This tabernacle is a type of the New Testament church. It is also a type of the apostolic. It was a tent erected by David to house the Ark of the Covenant. Courses of priests were set in place to praise the Lord continually. Many of the psalms were birthed and written during this time. These psalms were prophetic and declared the will and purposes of God.

David was a prophetic psalmist. The church should be prophetic in worship. New songs should be released continually. Every time God does something new, he releases new songs (Isaiah 42:9-10). Anointed minstrels release new sounds that move the hand of God (2 Kings 3:15). The development and release of psalmists and minstrels is a key part of restoring the Tabernacle of David.

Apostolic churches will be known for the presence of God. There will be a greater liberty and degree of glory in these churches that will affect the spirits of the people. A major part of releasing that glory is the release of anointed psalmists and minstrels. The Church must be taught the importance of the manifest presence of God. Believers must know how the presence of God affects and changes a person. Our spirits are impacted and activated as we come into contact with God's glory.

The music of the church must be strong and penetrating. The minstrels that have been exposed to the apostolic anointing will have a liberty and strength to release the proper sounds that bring deliverance and move the hand of God. The music cannot be weak, religious, and traditional. We are not building traditional churches, but prototype churches.

This is an important part of training and strengthening the spirits of the people. When the spirits of the people are activated and opened up through anointed praise and worship, they will be in a position to receive and understand the revelation that God is releasing. Their spirits will be activated and tuned to a higher frequency. They will be able to receive and walk in deeper truth. They will be able to handle the strong meat of the Word.

Apostolic churches will also be known by their liberty. The restraints of religion and tradition are broken. Dancing, praising, shouting, and celebrating are normal. Prophetic utterances are released. New songs are birthed and sung. People are free to enjoy and experience the presence of God. Praise and worship is not just a song service to allow extra time for all the people to arrive, or to prepare to hear a twenty-minute sermon. Praise and worship must be a vital part of the church.

The people will experience what it is to live under an open heaven. The apostolic anointing has the ability to open the heavens and keep them open. Apostles have a grace to connect with heaven's resources and pull them down to the earth for ministry function. It is refreshing to live under an open heaven. The Church becomes the gate of heaven (Genesis 28:17). Through this gate, the Lord pours His blessings upon the people.

Our church was radically affected by the ministry of Pastor Tom Bynum. His prophetic psalmist anointing helped release us into a new dimension of praise and worship. There is no substitute for anointed psalmists and praise leaders. Apostolic leaders cannot be satisfied with traditional singing and the usual praise and worship. We must be a part of the rebuilding of the Tabernacle of David. David released prophetic priests to be in charge of the worship (1 Chronicles 25:1-5). Apostles are anointed to establish. David established the order of worship for the nation of Israel. Although an Old Testament man, he was able to taste the powers of the age to come (Hebrews 6:5). We can also taste the powers of the age to come. David was able to receive a revelation from heaven and establish it upon the earth.

Apostolic churches are Judah churches. Judah means praise. These churches will have their hand in the neck of the enemy. They will carry a scepter of authority. The people will gather into these churches because of the open heaven and glory that results (Genesis 49:8-10). The results of rebuilding the Tabernacle of David will be possessing the land and the nations seeking God (Amos 8:11-12).

Chapter 9
Apostolic Functions

Leaders who are making the transition from a pastoral to an apostolic mode need to understand the functions of the apostolic ministry. Some apostolic anointings function differently from pastoral anointings (apostolic anointings that are different or that are in addition to pastoral anointings). The duties of the apostle that need to be executed and carried out are numerous. When leaders understand the various functions of this ministry, they will be able to fully move into this ministry, and there will be a grace to fulfill these functions and faithfully carry them out. The following are some of the functions of apostles:

1. Apostles pioneer.
2. Apostles plant churches.
3. Apostles ordain elders.
4. Apostles reform and bring change.
5. Apostles teach, preach, and set doctrine.
6. Apostles release revelation concerning the plans and purposes of God.
7. Apostles raise up and establish teams.
8. Apostles oversee churches.
9. Apostles confirm and strengthen local churches.
10. Apostles bring judgment and correction.
11. Apostles defend the faith.

12. Apostles gather.
13. Apostles establish.
14. Apostles lay foundation.
15. Apostles root out, tear down, throw down, destroy, build, and plant.
16. Apostles water.
17. Apostles bless the poor.
18. Apostles help perfect the saints.
19. Apostles release and activate.
20. Apostles impart.
21. Apostles help release the fullness of the Holy Spirit.
22. Apostles bring strategies to the church.
23. Apostles operate in signs, wonders, and miracles.
24. Apostles declare and decree.
25. Apostles remit sins.

Apostles must operate in faith and know that they are anointed to carry out the different functions of this ministry. This will cause them to expand and launch out into a broader and wider sphere of ministry. More people will be influenced and blessed by the anointing that is released through an apostolic ministry. It is a stronger anointing that carries a greater degree of power and authority. As the apostle steps into this ministry by faith, there will be new dimensions of grace made available.

The gifts of God operate by faith. The more confidence and faith a person walks in, the more manifestations of the Spirit he/she will experience. Doubt and passivity will prevent you from walking in the fullness of your calling. Most ministers live and die without entering into all the phases of their ministry. Instead of exceeding their boundaries, many never explore and possess their God given perimeters. These gifts will be dormant until stirred up by faith (2 Timothy 1:6).

Enlarge the place of thy tent, and let them stretch forth the curtains of thine habitations: spare not, lengthen thy cords, and strengthen thy stakes;

For thou shalt break forth on the right hand and on the left; and thy seed shall inherit the Gentiles, and make the desolate cities to be inhabited.

Isaiah 54:2-3

This is a prophetic word for this hour. It is time to enlarge the place of thy tent. Your tent represents your area of ministry. It is time to lengthen your cords and strengthen your stakes. God is calling you to a greater area of ministry. The areas mentioned in this book must be strengthened in the local church. It is up to the leaders to do the enlarging.

To *enlarge* means to increase the capacity or scope of. It means to expand. Too many leaders are confining themselves to the four walls of a local church. Many will die within those walls if they do not enlarge. The move from the pastoral to the apostolic is an enlargement. It is an expansion that will result in a greater capacity to receive and handle all that God is releasing. Many ministries are about to break forth on both sides. They will not be able to handle this breaking forth if they do not make room.

Our spirits must be enlarged. Our visions must increase. The apostolic anointing always enlarges and stretches the vision of the Church. This office will challenge and stir leaders to do more. It will expand your borders and extend your line throughout the earth (Psalm 19:4). It will break the limitations of culture and tradition, and it will launch leaders beyond their present boundaries.

Unto him that has shall more be given; and unto him that hath not, from him shall be taken even that which he hath.

Mark 4:25

God is releasing more to those who have revelation and are willing to make the shift. Those who refuse to change will lose what they have. Shifting and changing is necessary if we are to continue to walk in the blessing of God.

As I travel and minister to leaders and churches around the world, I am excited to see what is happening in the lives of leaders and members alike. We have been ordaining leaders as apostles in several, different nations. Ordination by man is not necessary to function as an apostle. However, many leaders need the confirmation and recognition by proven apostolic leaders. Jesus ordained the twelve (Mark 3:14). There will be apostles that ordain and release other apostles. This helps to release and thrust them into the call.

This is an exciting time to be alive! God is breaking the limitations off of our lives and releasing us into our destinies! My desire is to see leaders and churches come into the fullness of what God has ordained. Let us not live beneath our privilege. Let us rise up and embrace everything that our Lord died and shed His blood to purchase for us. We will bring pleasure to God and displeasure to the devil.

May grace and peace be multiplied unto the Church of Jesus Christ!

References

Cannastraci, David. *Apostles and the Emerging Apostolic Movement.* Ventura: Renew Books, 1996.

David, Jonathan. *Apostolic Strategies Affecting Nations.* Muar: Full Gospel Centre, 1999.

Eckhardt, John. *Apostolic Ministry (A 50 Lesson Bible Course).* Oak Park: Crusaders Ministries, 2005.

---. *Moving in the Apostolic.* Ventura: Renew Books, 1999.

---. *The Ministry Anointing of the Apostle.* Chicago: Crusaders Ministries, 1993.

---. *Fifty Truths Concerning Apostolic Ministry.* Chicago: Crusaders Ministries, 1998.

---. *The Apostolic Church.* Chicago: Crusaders Ministries, 1996.

---. *Presbyteries and Apostolic Teams.*

Sapp, Roger. *The Last Apostles on Earth.* Shippensburg: Companion Press, 1995.

For Ministry Information and/or
Book and Tape Orders
Please Contact:

CRUSADERS MINISTRIES
P.O. Box 492
Matteson, IL 60443
(708) 922-0983